A Respectful Lady
and a
Southern Gentleman

A Respectful Lady

and a

Southern Gentleman

Melanie S. Padgett

PALMETTO
P U B L I S H I N G
Charleston, SC
www.PalmettoPublishing.com

Copyright © 2024 by Melanie S. Padgett

All rights reserved

No portion of this book may be reproduced, stored in a retrieval system, or transmitted in any form by any means–electronic, mechanical, photocopy, recording, or other–except for brief quotations in printed reviews, without prior permission of the author.

Paperback ISBN: 979-8-8229-5715-2

Contents

Acknowledgements vii
Chapter 1   God Provides 1
Chapter 2   My Heart's Desire. 3
Chapter 3   My Family Meets My Sweetheart 5
Chapter 4   A Change in Our Friendship 8
Chapter 5   Married Life 10
Chapter 6   COVID 23
Chapter 7   Pray Hard 33
Chapter 8   Summary 35
Credits 39

Acknowledgements

To say "Thank you," to my Sweetheart, Vaughn Padgett, for the time God allowed us to be married is something I have done countless times; both while he was living with me as my husband, and now as he is living in Heaven. How I thank God that he showed us and told us he loved us in so many ways. Thank you, LORD Jesus for answering my prayers. Vaughn was one of the answers in the sweetest and most marvelous of Thy ways.

Thank you, Ms. Eldora "Janette" Williams, my former school principal, who, when I mentioned to about writing, encouraged me "To write that book,"

Thank you, Mrs. Curlenia McMahon, for being my friend, prayer guide and first reader of this book. Every time we can be together, your joy in the LORD Jesus is so contagious; uplifting me to be more like Him.

Thank you, Mrs. Jane Miles, and Pastor Bill Monroe: Secretary to and Preacher to Florence Baptist Temple; my Pastor, home church and church family. Thank you for reading the book, then taking the time to counsel, and give me good direction. Pastor, your godly insight gave me the assurance to move forward to complete it.

Thank you to my children: Regent, McCall, Seir, Teil and CJ; ya'll are and continue to be the greatest proof that God answers prayers. In just about every way I can think of, God has poured out His love for me by allowing me to be your mother. I continue to want to love and grow in Christ everyday because of His gift of motherhood to me by all of you. I love you all so much. Mama

To Sawyer and Zoe: Your Granddaddy was a wonderful man, who loved and served our Lord Jesus, and loved us every minute of the time we were with him. His love for both of you, even before your birth, was evident by his fervent prayers for you. I know because I was there and heard him yearn to God in prayer for you. You both are an answer to our prayers. I love you both. Grandma Melanie

CHAPTER 1

God Provides

Phil 4:13 But, my God shall supply all your need according to His riches in glory by Christ Jesus.

In the fall of 2007, while cooking dinner, a friend of mine called. She said the Lord was doing a work in her life. She further explained what she meant by, telling me she heard the sermon last Sunday preached at our church: "Giving." Through the Bible message, the Spirit of God convicted her of overspending. Her and her husband had an extra vehicle they did not use. She wanted to sell it and give the money from the sales to someone in need. She prayed about her conviction and asked God to work on her husband's heart. She wanted to talk to him, and needed him to be understanding and agreeable with her. After a heartfelt prayer, she went about her duties; cleaning the house and preparing dinner for her family. As they ate the meal prepared that evening, her husband began to tell her, he felt like they needed to get rid of the extra truck they had and use the money to help someone else.

She was excited! While I stirred my pot of spaghetti sauce, we shared in the joy of how God answers prayers. We prayed about what God would do next.

My friend continued the story from the week's prayers. She put a "For Sale" sign on the truck, and parked it in a busy location of town. They tried selling the car, but the week went by with no luck. A lady did call, and made an offer, but they did not have a "peace" about the suggested sales price and her offer, so they continued to pray and wait.

By this time, fall had left and winter settled in. It was a new year, but the same prayer. A storm came into town and the city of Macon stood in shambles. With torn down trees, a Georgia power worker saw the couples' "For Sale" sign. He inquired of the price, was agreeable and paid cash for the car; right on the spot. With the cash in tow; the reason for the phone call. My friend wanted to give me money to buy a dependable car. I could not believe my ears! As I deciphered all this amazing information, I thanked God and my friend. The next day, I told my Daddy about getting money to buy a newer car. Since my Daddy's the best dealer-mechanic, and knows everything about a car. I asked his advice. He told me his neighbor just happened to have a van for sale. He wanted me to come by and take a look. Both of us went and inspected the van. Daddy checked all the parts and I glanced at the shape, size, and look of it, as I test drove it around the block. Throughout this process, God provided me a new car.

CHAPTER 2

My Heart's Desire

Psalm 37:4 Delight thyself also in the Lord;
and He shall give thee the desires of thy heart.

In the spring of 2008, God prompted my heart to pray for a husband. I began to pray for God to bring His person-His man into my life. I sat my children down and talked to them, telling them all that was on my heart. We prayed together and I joined an online dating service. The program matches you to other possible relationships by matching personality profiles. I chose the more restricted plan which includes email contact but not large photo spaces or personal information. I saw Vaughn's picture as a possible match. What I saw, was a man filled with joy; his smile and light, kind eyes. He was with children; stooping down on their level showing tenderness and care. In another, he was serving food to children. Another; he was outside in nature. The pictures were all I knew, but they drew me in to take a closer look. We began communicating by asking and answering each other's questions; either given by the dating service, or ones we picked out personally to ask and answer. I readily answered his questions concerning my Salvation experience, life verses from God's Word –the Bible, and my thoughts of a southern gentleman and a respectable lady. I told him, "I like your questions!" He said, "I like your answers!" We began to feel a sweet connection in the Lord.

Our first phone conversation began on a voicemail. Vaughn was walking his daughter's dog. Out of breath, Vaughn called me back. Except for the week of him going to Mexico on a church mission trip, God has allowed us to talk daily either by phone, text messages, or emails. We established prayer in the beginning of our relationship. God has been so faithful to us in prayer. He hears us and answers our petitions. He accepts our praises. He has been our mainstay and our anchor. We agreed that praying together regularly would draw us together as one. God would show us how to walk as a couple now. God has established the Power of His Word in our lives through reading the Bible each day. He has been with Vaughn and I, speaking to us through His Word, training us in daily practice and guiding us to serve Him; forgive others and give faithfully. God's Word never fails.

It was Vaughn that God spoke to about us reading His Word together. We used a Bible reading plan to read through the Bible in one year. We wanted our hearts open to hear from God as a couple and continue to build our hearts as one. We knew it was God's perfect plan for us to be together.

CHAPTER 3

My Family Meets My Sweetheart

Psalm 75:1 Unto Thee, O God, do we give thanks,
unto Thee do we give thanks, for that Thy Name is near
Thy wondrous works declare.

After several emails and phone calls, there was not a day that went by that we did not talk in the morning and in the evening. In the morning, we would talk about our Bible reading and what God spoke to us about, and in the evening, we would discuss our day and pray together. This continued throughout the summer months. Then, football season hit. I found out, being a resident of South Carolina, my sweetheart loves his Clemson Tigers! He lived on the Clemson campus as a boy when his dad, Adrian Padgett went to school there. His parents lived on campus in the married housing provided, while Vaughn rode his bike to the football stadium; gazing in awe at the fans and athletes. He watched the "Tiger" parade. His excitement was contagious! He attended the football games every year; memorizing stats and characteristics of the players and coaches. He wore orange and purple every chance he got. It would only make sense for him to want me to be a part of his weekend fun.

Vaughn invited me to my first Clemson football game. Before the game, he came to my house for lunch. Also with him, was his daughter and neighbor. Our home was buzzing with Mama and the kids all around; not to mention our dog. While waiting for lunch, one daughter munched on a turkey sandwich, and my son played checkers with Vaughn's neighbor. With everyone seemingly "settled," my Mama wanted to ask Vaughn a few questions. She wanted to know why my sweetheart had joined an online dating service. From an earlier conversation, she already knew my story. Vaughn explained to her, he saw a commercial about a free weekend. He said, "Unlike Melanie, who had this all planned and thought out; I just saw the television ad and said "Why not?" He then expounded, "The reason God has Melanie and me together today is because of this table where we are sitting: my grandmother's table. I saw a picture of Melanie sitting here with her Bible, pen and journal. It was just like me! After our short visit, we headed to Atlanta for the season opener of Clemson football against Alabama. We left "ticketless!" Vaughn decided early on that not having tickets would be no problem (I had no idea of this idea until we were in Atlanta). We arrived in Atlanta early. We walked around downtown peach city with Clemson orange fans and crimson diehards. Vaughn, and me walked around Olympic Park greeting fellow Clemson addicts; showing respect to all and striking up conversations with new acquaintances.

Our daughter sent text messages to her aunts and a host of friends. We settled down on the picnic area in a soft grassy spot to watch the game on the large outdoor screen. We held a "Need 4 Tickets" sign. A Clemson man walked to us and asked if we were Clemson fans. With that assurance, he sold us the tickets face value. We were only able to secure three tickets. Vaughn's friend went to a nearby restaurant and watched the game while we walked into the stadium. Vaughn and I sat together while his daughter sat in the row in front of us. Go Tigers!

The season opener was a loss to Alabama (who later went on to have a 12-0 season losing only to Florida and Oklahoma), but our first Clemson game together was a "huge success!" God had so sweetly brought us a common interest to share and have fun. We showed our gratefulness to Him by attending Sunday worship the next day. We sat side-by-side, along with our family. Our time at church was a blessing.

CHAPTER 4

A Change in Our Friendship

Psalm 98:1a O, sing unto the LORD a new song;
for He hath done marvelous things.

I must mention a highlight in our dating relationship. While sitting in the car in Macon before the game, waiting on Betsy and Larry to arrive; we had a moment together. We anticipated this moment alone to share our true feelings. Vaughn took his ipod and began playing a song, and singing along. The song "I Only Have Eyes for You" was a 70's classic. Vaughn said he loved me face to face. I gazed into his beautiful green eyes and told him I loved him, too. It was electric! I felt so loved. Vaughn told me those endearing words, "You are so precious." I felt "precious" in his eyes.

We ate lunch after church. Vaughn, Betsy and Larry had to head back to Florence. We embraced and joyfully kissed having experienced a wonderful weekend and marveling at what God had done for us.

A Change in Our Friendship

Soon, more Clemson dates followed. Our pattern was to meet in Clemson, South Carolina before the Saturday game. I would drive from Macon-Atlanta while Vaughn came across the state of South Carolina from Florence to Clemson. We met at Cracker Barrel all smiles eager to hold hands. We brought each other gifts and shared travel stories. We talked about the week's family experiences, church services, and gave prayer and praise reports. Vaughn bought me a Scofield Study Bible-King James Version. I call it the "Gold Bible" because of its fancy gold edging on the pages. It is the Word of our Living God, Jesus Christ our Savior. Each morsel is read, received, understood, and practiced-like gold. It is the highest treasure we can live by. We have such victory living day by day in the love of Jesus. It is also the Bible I use today, every morning, to read and communicate to our Lord and Savior Jesus Christ. I read and ask Him to open my heart to hear what He is saying and then help me obey His words of grace and peace.

CHAPTER 5

Married Life

It still amazes me today, 13 years later, that we became husband and wife. We moved to Florence, South Carolina. My teaching job began in the late summer of 2009 with the Florence One School District. Vaughn's household quickly changed from a single man to a wife and family.

The best way to give you an idea of how God was working, is for me to give you a peek into our letters, cards and notes to each other.

The next few pages are copies of letters and notes I wrote to my sweetheart during our day to day activities. I hope it will give you a glimpse into the special man I married.

Tuesday 11/4/14

Dear Sweetheart,

I just wanted to take a minute to tell you how much I love you, and how much I am thankful to God for you. You are a nice husband to me, I notice how you smile when you look at me, and you let me talk to you when you are trying to rest after a long day at work. You answer the phone when I call you and you let me talk to you while you are at work. You have a willing attitude because you always give me easy answers. It is a praise to God we agree so much!

Your love for our children astonishes me. I never knew someone could or would care for the children with me as much as me. You have proven yourself as loving time and time again by the way you give to them. You listen them, teach them the Bible, and respond to their complaints and behavior by giving them Biblically sound counsel. You correct them as a loving father. They listen and obey you.

I am glad and content and settled being your wife. Thank you for letting me stay home today, clean house, read and work in the yard. You let me do things I enjoy and you do not pressure me.

Thank you for reading the Bible to me every morning, praying with me and for me, the children and our coworkers. It is a joy to plan our lives for how God wants our future. I look forward to how He will use us to bear much fruit for

Him; not only for our family, but at our jobs, our church in ministry to build Eternity.

I love you sweetheart,

Your Mrs. Joy (I acquired that name because I called my husband my Mr. Joy" because he was a joy filled man that loved to smile and sing. I gazed at him often and the name fit).6.

Fathers Day 2010

Darling,

It means the world to me that you are in our lives. You love us and take up time with all of us. You give so much; especially the sacrifices on the Macon house (I still had a house in Macon, Ga. We had renters at the time. Vaughn would check on the house and make any necessary repairs). I love the way you love the kids; and the Macon girls, and our daughter in South Carolina. It warms my heart to watch you show our son so much of your life.

January 20, 2014

Dear Vaughn,

Thank you for taking such care of me and the kids. I am very grateful for how you feed our dog, going outside in the cold at night to check on her. You stay up for our daughter if she needs a ride so I can go to bed and rest. Thank you for driving to Macon. I thank God for how nice you are to me. I especially am encouraged by your patience with our young son. You teach him and talk to him about better things. You go to his ballgames. You lift me up by reading the Bible every morning and walk me to a warmed up car. You pray with me and the children every night. You listen to me. I do not ever want to remember when or have to live without you in the future. Only my love and dependence on Jesus is greater. It is a joy to be your wife, and lover and friend.

I love you.

Your Mrs. Joy

June 6, 2014: 5 wonderful years of joy!"
Sweetheart (from me),

You are as dear to me today, as the fist time I saw you with your arms open wide and bright smile at the green pastures (the green pastures is a place we termed that is a grassy area in the city of Florence).

July 30, 2014

Vaughn's birthday

Sweetheart,

You are a blessing to me every day.

May 13, 2016
Ephesians 4:32 And be ye kind one to another.

Sweetheart,

Thank you for being the model of kindness; taking the time to bring me a "coke" at school-right when I needed a lift (you coming to see me was the "treat"); the pizza you bought us for dinner (after a long work day), and all the while, serving and honoring your parents in love and faithfulness.

I love you.

Your Mrs. Joy

March 24, 2016

Sweetheart,

For the Lord God is a sun and a shield. The Lord will give grace and glory; no good thing will he withhold from them that walk uprightly.
    Oh, Lord of hosts, blessed is the man that trusts in thee. Psalm 84: 11-12
    I prayed for you this morning.

Your Mrs. Joy

Fathers Day 2016

Thank you sweetheart-

Cars, cars, cars (me and yours and our kids)-

    For the loving kindness you put in caring for all the children at each area of need in their lives. I really appreciate your dedication and cooperation to our family-so we can truly be a family.

March 24, 2017,

Dear Sweetheart,

I just wanted to tell you how much I appreciate you. You give so much at work-working hard to create peace and goodness in your job. For our family, you give to me and the kids out of your abundance to make sure we have what we need. You are thoughtful always to me in loving ways. Thank you.

April 16, 2017

Sweetheart,

As pretty as I think these flowers are on the front of the card, and as nice as it has been to have a day to be at home, and as pleasant as getting things done around the house, or catching up on work responsibilities…nothing compares to being with you. I am very thankful for Easter-for Christ and my relationship with Him. I am very thankful for His love that flows through you to me. I have come to depend on your love for everything. I need you. Thank you for being here and depending on our Lord and Savior to see us through.

I love you.

Your Mrs. Joy

January 4, 2018

Thank you, sweetheart for being the sweetest husband. I love you.

Dear Sweetheart,

I just wanted to say thank you again for putting up the ceiling fans. Thank you for making our home look nice and an inviting place to come home to every night. I have enjoyed the time to sit and admire your handiwork. I praise and thank God for you, for your love for Him, your love for me, our children and our family.

May 31, 2018

Sweetheart,

Thank you for working so hard in the yard this weekend. Your hard work is why our yard and house are a nice place to come home to. Thank you.

Your Mrs. Joy

November 16, 2018

I thank God you want to grow as His Son by reading your Bible and having time to learn and hear from God each day. How could I have gotten such a good husband? I know because of God's love for us. He answers our prayers. I know God is faithful and will continue to be with us and teach us in these days ahead.

Love, Your Mrs. Joy

June 6, 2018

9 wonderful years of marriage Happy Anniversary

Mr. Joy,

I really thought about finding you something copper (traditional anniversary gift is copper for 9 yrs of marriage). I thought of the pennies (I gave him 9 pennies taped to the card) because of the children I teach and we minister to; something so simple, yet has much meaning to us.

I love you sweetheart, Your Mrs. Joy

Fathers Day 2018

Sweetheart,

Psalm 112:5 A good man shows favor, lends, and guides his affairs with discretion. I've seen you do this over and over again.

Proverb 22:1 A good name is rather to be chosen than great riches and loving favor rather than silver or gold. Love, Your Mrs. Joy

---

Sept. 20, 2018

The memory of the just is blessed. Proverbs 10:7 Most men will proclaim everyone his own goodness, but a faithful man who can find? The just man walketh in his integrity: his children are blessed after him. Proverbs 20:6-7

Sweetheart,

What a joy to my heart to sing praises of confidence (we are more than conquerors in Christ Jesus) last night with the children. I praise God because He brought me to you to live as you are living; an example to me and so many others, too. I have asked God to forgive me for resisting-at times-your opinions and ideas for our joy and growth. I am certain of your love for me because you have sacrificed at those times by showing love to me and expecting nothing in return. My prayer and then my doing in Christ is to double that love back to you every day God gives us as husband and wife.

I love you.

Your Mrs. Joy

May 11, 2020

Thank you, sweetheart. The Olive Garden lunch was very nice (my mother's day gift). The lasagna was a great choice. I really enjoyed it. Thank you for all you did to pay for it and cooperate with our family (our children's idea to do this). I appreciate your willingness to help the kids with all the planning, implementing, and driving to get the meal and bring it to the house (COVID has hit and restaurants are not taking customers inside their stores). You were so nice to heat it up, too.

June 6, 2020

Our 11th wedding anniversary. COVID is in full bloom.

Sweetheart, Happy is the man that finds wisdom. A faithful man shall abound with blessings. I praise God for His way in your life and thank God you married me.

I love you.

Your Mrs. Joy

July 30, 2022 Vaughn's 65th birthday

Sweetheart, I saw the front of this card (it is a picture of flowers reminding me of the beautiful flower pictures he takes with his camera), and could've kept looking at the cover indefinitely. You are a wonderful person, a wonderful son, and husband and father, and neighbor to all. I wish you a happy birthday today. I am glad to get to share it with you. Happy Birthday. I love you Sweetheart.

Love, Your Mrs. Joy

CHAPTER 6

COVID

My sweetheart meekly put his whole heart into assisting me with my classroom. Teaching a self contained autistic Kindergarten class was no small feat, and having my husband's 100% support helped. He prayed for me and with me for my students, assistant teachers, coworkers, leaders, supervisors, parents and families. Vaughn wrote me notes of encouragement. He dropped by the school with small gifts for me. All of these languages of love strengthened me and filled me with joy. I knew how much I was loved by him. Subsequently, I also knew how much I was loved by God because He brought me such love through a willing servant. Vaughn made many willing sacrifices for me, my assistants and my students. He bought needed school supplies and sensory items for the children. He bought donuts every Friday for one whole year for my assistants and other teachers sharing in the responsibility for training the children.

One particular note I have kept, Vaughn wrote "Your Mr. Joy loves you." It is written on the back of a document letter with a bold red marker. I place the note in the front of my teacher notebook, for thirteen years. Every time I open the notebook to take notes in staff meetings, I see the precious words and think on those things.

Vaughn was a thoughtful husband; often purchasing store bought cards for my birthday. In one particular card on 10/14/2019, Vaughn wrote "I am so blessed to have you in my life. I love you. Your Mr. Joy." And in another, "I love you, Sweetheart. Your Mr. Joy."

Christmas 2019 came and I was given an interesting card. With all he gave me of himself, I was a little troubled in spirit when I read these Christmas words.

As I look back on things, I believe God was preparing me for the year ahead. The Christmas card reads "Sweetheart, I may not know what to get you, or when to get it. I do know I love you with all my heard. I will never leave you or forsake you. Please forgive me. Your Mr. Joy

My life verses. Hebrews 13:5-6. Our first words together. Little did anyone know, COVID would hit America strong and fast.

When the news came from my Principal, Janette Williams, that school would be out for a few weeks, I was not alarmed. The teachers were told that COVID 19 was in epidemic proportions around the country and our school system, Florence One Schools, would be closed for a few weeks until it passed by, and things got clear and back to normal. Little did anyone know how true that to be.

I gathered up my things, packed some homework for the children, and went home to sit. I sat for 3 weeks waiting to hear from our community leaders. My church even shut down for some time. I knew things must be very serious. At this point, I was still in contact with my children and parents, and most of my family. My sweetheart continued to go to work every day. His job did not shut down. Each worker clocked in and out daily, continuing to work in the mechanical and insulation business. Vaughn had a big job, as he called it, and went daily across town to the job site. Each morning, someone would take his temperature. With signs of COVID being a high temperature, some workers were sent home to quarantine for a certain amount of days until the symptoms did not exist. Usually, a cough was persistent and breathing was difficult. My husband continued to work.

It was difficult to find some store supplies, so he would go to a variety of stores to get groceries or toiletries. Supplies were getting hard to find.

The days turned into weeks and months. Soon school was out. The children or faculty had not returned to the building. COVID was still in full force and it was too much of a risk to be in close contact with a group of people. Our church had an outside service to bring us together. Our pastor, from the very beginning, began online services. He was often, beside the camera crew and a few of the pastoral staff, the only person in the church building. How lonely or helpless he must have felt. He was an example to me of pressing on in faith. He wore little bracelet (and perhaps, still does) on his wrist with those words. Such meaningful words meant much to me.

Our former Sunday School teacher, David and is wife Anita held a "Zoom" class each week for online Bible Study and prayer, Vaughn did not miss one. How thankful to God we were to be in His Word with other believers.

June 2020 was our 11th wedding anniversary. Never in 1000 years did I realize it would be our last. Vaughn, again, wrote words from a store bought card, and presented it to me. The words would encourage me in the trying days to come. "With all my heart, Happy Anniversary. My love for you, my Sweetheart, grows with each new day. The best times for us are yet to come. Your Mr. Joy."

The new school year would start after Labor Day this year. Our leaders wanted to make sure COVID was weakened. Many people chose to continue staying at home, preferring the choice to home school, or opt for the online school choice. Teachers were hired for both online and at the school building. My class was to be held in person at Lester School. Vaughn was such a great handyman and could build, fix and repair anything. His engineering skills were used to help people we knew that needed ceiling fans installed in their homes, appliance repair, plumbing problems and overall home improvement. Vaughn made himself available anytime anyone asked for his help. He was glad to do it.

At this point, our church also was getting back into the building. It was September 2020. Vaughn saw a need in our classroom. I asked his counsel to build shields for my 2 classroom assistants; Ms. Bonnie and Ms. Danah. The school furnished one shield for my desk. We needed 2 more. Vaughn looked at our Christian school and took a picture of the shields made for them. He went to his work warehouse and designed similar style for Danah and Bonnie. How we would have been heart broken if one of them got COVID, from exposure in our classroom. Many times Vaughn prayed for me and the teachers at Lester, that God would protect us.

We were very excited to be back at church, serving in the children's ministry. Our Christian school started and our families were slowly but surely returning to worship and serve God. Things were beginning to look like they might get back to the way they were.

On September 3rd (Wednesday), Vaughn sent me a text message saying he did not feel well, and that he had a persistent cough. He did not think it was good idea for him to go to church that evening, because it might alarm others or he might be contagious. He came home and rested. When I got home, noticed him lying on the floor. When I asked him why he was not in bed, he said he did not want to infect me. His cough was beginning to cause him pain. It was frequent, especially when talking, so he succumbed to texting family and close friends.

Our pastor had asked all of the congregation to pray. He made a prayer schedule for our church, Florence Baptist Temple. We were instructed to sign up on the church website www.fbt.org. Our time was 5:30 pm. We decided that was best for us; to pray before we eat our evening meal.

On Saturday, September 6th, 2020 I woke up with a fever. I was very tired. I figured it was because of the teacher workdays and extra measures of getting the classroom "COVID" ready. There were masks to wear, constant washing of hands, placing furniture 6 feet apart, putting shields on desks, and a lot of extra wiping down shelves and furniture for cleanliness. Our school district was taking measures outlined by The Department of Health. Nurses were under pressure to keep and produce all the latest information. People were concerned and rightly so. People were dying from COVID 19 in the United States, and the numbers were rising. Vaughn and I drove to the nearest COVID test center, our local hospital. We both had COVID 19. We were told to quarantine, stay inside and 6 feet apart, and notify others we had been in contact with. We both lost our appetites and did not want to eat much. I had diarrhea and a constant stomach ache. I could not eat. A friend of mine suggested yogurt. Mrs. Belinda, my friend from church, brought me a whole Food Lion bag filled with small individual containers of yogurt. In a variety of flavors. The yogurt tasted good, was smooth on my digestion and I felt better. Our Sunday School teacher, Steve called Vaughn every day to check on his progress. Earlier, our class had tried to get together for a small fellowship at a local barbeque place in town. With masks and gloves in tow, we ate a meal together. It was encouraging to both of us to have a meal and fellowship with our church family. It was a strange time for all of us to go through. It affected everyone in some way or another. Before the 10th day of quarantine, my husband's cough continued and his breathing more labored. He made the decision on Saturday, September 13th to call the ambulance and have them drive him to the hospital. I wanted to go with him but the paramedics would not let me go since I also, had COVID and would infect others.

Having Vaughn leave the house without me was hard on both of us. But, Vaughn put me at ease when he sent me a text message, stating he was getting medicine and fluids. He already felt his appetite coming back. He told me "We did the right thing." I called our family and our church and asked for their prayers. I know many people prayed for my sweetheart: his daughter and son-law, his step children, our family, friends, coworkers, Christian brothers and sisters, our Pastor, the church staff, and our neighbors were all praying for Vaughn. I will never know how many people prayed for Vaughn, until I get to Heaven, however, I am very grateful.

During his hospital stay, no one could visit him. There were very strict COVID guidelines at the time. Many people still were contacting the virus and having to be quarantined. Surrounding South Carolina cities and counties were taking measures to keep our state "safe."

Each morning, after reading my Bible, I felt God's comfort and took His words to heart. I communicated them every morning to my husband, so he would fill to full. One particular morning, on September 18th, I read the 18th Proverb. In verse 10, the Bible says, "The Name of the LORD is a strong tower, the righteous run into it and is safe." I told Vaughn those words, not realizing how important they would be in the hours ahead that day.

Little did I know, at 1:00 pm he would be put on a ventilator. I found out by his text. Around 3:15 pm the same day, his doctor called me. He said, your husband has gone into cardiac arrest. We have brought him back. My first thought, if he was brought back to life, it was from God Almighty. I thanked God. I called Betsy. I called my Mama. I was finally given permission to go to the hospital and see my sweetheart, after being apart five days; the longest we have ever been apart since our marriage.

Our pastor was called and the pastoral staff. They had been praying for Vaughn everyday. Someone from the staff or the deacons called me everyday and prayed with me. How thankful I am to God for them.

The next days were minute by minute. So many people that love Vaughn were praying for him. I could not name them all. God had mercy on us because He gave precious days for Betsy to call her daddy and talk to him. Even though, Vaughn had been given medicine to stay asleep, we were living by faith he would hear us. Betsy played music, prayed for her daddy and read the Bible to him. I thought of the Bible verse in Hebrews 11:1 "Now faith, is the substance of things hoped for, the evidence of things not seen."

My sweetheart went home to be with the Lord, on Monday, September 28th 2020 at 3:59 pm.

In the days to come, I received many cards in the mail with notes of comfort.

Here are 2 very special ones that I believe honor "Mr. Adrian Vaughn Padgett:" Here is a part on one such card:

Melanie, Vaughn had a servant's heart, His love for others inspires me to do more, His love for Christ challenges me to do more for His Kingdom. Years ago, Vaughn was my kids choir teacher. He was so faithful. We will miss him! We are praying for you and your family. Thank you for your service to FBT and our LORD. I am thank you for the influence Vaughn had on my life. Press on in Faith!

FBT Member

Dear Mrs. Padgett,

As I write this letter, I can't begin to express how sad we feel; the shock few are enduring is far beyond measure. But know, now and always you and your family are in our prayers. We grieve with you. Thank God for Jesus and how you have allowed Him to be your refuge and strength, an ever present help in trouble (Ps 46:1). Thank God for your Salvation because it comes from Him. We loved Mr. Padgett. He was such a blessing during our son's illness. We thank God for him and the way he shared Christ with others. Be faithful even to the point of death, and I will give you a crown of life (Rev. 2:10). Thank God for Mr. Padgett sharing prayers, praises and God's Word with us.

These are just a few words (not the entire letters) to give you a picture of the gentleman I married.

May God Bless you.

Sincerely,

Melanie Padgett
Vaughn's Mrs. Joy
August 17, 2022

CHAPTER 7

Pray Hard

Psalm 55:22 Cast thy burden upon the LORD, and he shall sustain thee: he shall never suffer the righteous to be moved.

Last words are very important. While in the hospital, the last words Vaughn said to me in a text message was to pray hard. Prayer would be our way of communication until the time of his death.

According to the Strong's Concordance, to pray means to communicate between others. It is an entreaty to ask someone to do something. In Genesis Chapter 12, while traveling to Egypt, Abraham asked his wife Sarah to tell the Egyptians she was his sister as soon as they got into town. Later in Genesis Chapter 19, Lot asked his neighbors not to do the wicked act they were set to do against his family and friends. In both cases, the word "pray" is used in the same way; to ask for something with urgency. I believe that is what my sweetheart meant when he told me to pray hard: God, please! Now!

Pray also means to intervene for someone; come to God in between Him and the person you are praying for. Talk to God for them. Another word is beseech: to hang on close because this is important to you. It can be as if you are "pulling" in our Lord Jesus and the virtues he holds.

Holding onto God's virtues gives me comfort. After my husband died, I was walking out of his hospital room. A young female nurse came to me and asked me, "Are you, Melanie?" I told her yes. She told me her name and that she was one of Vaughn's nurses. She said, "*Your sweetheart was a sweetheart.*" She continued by explaining that moments before he was put on the ventilator, he looked at her and said, "Are you a Christian? *Do you know the LORD?*" She said, "Yes, I am a Christian, and I do know Jesus as my Lord and Savior." Through tubes and cords, he reached his swollen hands to mine, asking me to pray with him. We prayed." She then said, "After our prayer, I looked into his eyes and saw his face. He was at peace. He smiled at me. His calm assurance witnessed to me of his faith in God. I remember how he trusted God and put his hope in Him." I left the hospital, trusting and hoping in God too.

CHAPTER 8

Summary

Through Vaughn's and my relationship, his illness and death, I have learned a few things: God's love for me, how to serve others, and how to share my faith. Vaughn showed his love for me very early in our meeting and times together; even before becoming his wife. He demonstrated it by telling me that he loved me often; even daily, and many times throughout the day. I did not ever wonder if he loved me because he told me repeatedly.

He lived a picture of how our Creator, God loves us. God has told us and tells us often; even daily, and many times throughout the day when we read the Bible, His Word to us. Vaughn spent time serving others: after a long work day, he would help people with their needs. He put in many hours updating and repairing others people's homes; even at the risk of his own home needing updates and repairs. He simply put the needs of family and friends first. I can remember one Christmas Day the phone rang around 10:00 am. A co-worker needed help installing a new sink, a gift for his wife. Vaughn gladly went and spent several hours taking care of this couple.

As mentioned in earlier chapters in this book, Vaughn served in our church in various ministries including the children's choir, kid worship, kids summer camp, adult Sunday School, Reformers Unanimous, and Self Confrontation. I grew spiritually because I saw him serve joyfully without complaint.

I learned to share my faith with others: giving the Gospel to friends and strangers alike. Vaughn talked to people about their spiritual beliefs. He made it look so easy. I asked him, "How can you tell people about Jesus' death, burial and resurrection, so easy?" Smiling, he said, "I just talk about Jesus!"

I now share my faith by just talking about Jesus! I say what was said by the apostle Paul in Acts 16:30 and 31 when asked the question by the keeper of the prison, "Sirs, what must I do to be saved? Believe on the Lord Jesus Christ, and you will be saved." If you do not know Jesus Christ as your personal Lord and Savior, you can: recognize your sin before God. He is Holy and just. Romans 3:23 says "For we have all sinned and come short of the glory of God."

Romans 6:23a "For the wages of sin is death."

Believe as the prison keeper did when the apostle Paul told him how to be saved. Ask God to forgive you of your sins. He is faithful and just to forgive you if you confess your sins. Romans 10:9-13 explains that if you confess with your mouth the Lord Jesus, and believe in your heart that God raised him from the dead, you will be saved.

I encourage you to get a Bible and read every day. Pray. Find and go to a church that has a preacher that preaches the Word, so you will hear it, have faith, and grow spiritually with other believers.

I pray you are blessed by reading this book.

God Bless you.

Credits

Chapter 1:

Philippians 4:19 But my God shall supply all you need according to his riches in glory by Christ Jesus.

The Scofield Study Bible King James Version 2003 Edition Editor C.I. Scofield, D.D. 1843–1921

Chapter 2:

Psalm 37:4 Delight thyself also in the LORD; and he shall give thee the desires of thine heart.

The Scofield Study Bible King James Version 2003 Edition Editor C.I. Scofield, D.D. 1843–1921

www.eharmony.com

Chapter 3:

Psalm 75:1 Unto thee, O God, do we give thanks, *unto thee* do we give thanks: for *that* thy name is near thy wondrous works declare.

The Scofield Study Bible King James Version 2003 Edition Editor C.I. Scofield, D.D. 1843–1921

Clemson University College Football Schedule 2008-9: Season opener game against The University of Alabama; Atlanta, GA. September 2008.

Chapter 4:

Psalm 98:1a O sing unto the LORD a new song; for he hath done marvelous things.

The Scofield Study Bible King James Version 2003 Edition Editor C.I. Scofield, D.D. 1843–1921

"I Only Have Eyes For You," sung by Art Garfunkle; Written by Harry Warren and Al Dubin, https://youtu.be/K9C53IEcg_0

The Scofield Study Bible King James Version 2003 Edition Editor C.I. Scofield, D.D. 1843–1921

Chapter 5:

Florence One Schools; https://www.f1s.org/Florence, South Carolina

Chapter 6:

Proverbs 18:10 The name of the LORD *is* a strong tower: the righteous runneth into it, and is safe.

Hebrews 11:1 Now faith is the substance of things hoped for, the evidence of things not seen.

The Scofield Study Bible King James Version 2003 Edition Editor C.I. Scofield, D.D. 1843-1921

Chapter 7:

Genesis 12: 10-13 Story of Abraham

Genesis 19: 1-7 Story of Lot

The Scofield Study Bible King James Version 2003 Edition Editor C.I. Scofield, D.D. 1843–1921

The Strongest Strong's Exhaustive Concordance of the Bible, James Strong, LL.D.

S.T.D. Fully Revised and Corrected by John R. Kohlenberger III and James A.

Swanson, Zondervan 2001, pray.

Chapter 8:

Carolina Insulation Contractors, 1416 Floyd Circle, Florence South Carolina 29501

Florence Baptist Temple, 2308 S Irby Street, Florence South Carolina, 29505

The Scofield Study Bible King James Version 2003 Edition Editor C.I. Scofield, D.D. 1843–1921

Acts 16:30-31, Romans 3:23, Romans 6:23a, Romans 10:9-13, 1John 1:9-10

My Darling Melanie,

There are things we share across the miles that make the distance seem small: God's word, God's stories of his Spirit working in our lives, seeing the same moon at night, and the same Clemson sky at morning and evening.

These love songs are some more things we can share together. They bring to my mind memories past, present and future. How can we have future memories? Remember when we talked about our first kiss and our first face-to-face, "I Love You?" Which was better: the anticipation of the memory, or the memory itself? May our future memories be so much better than the anticipated ones.

I Love You.

Your Mr. Joy,
Vaughn

www.ingramcontent.com/pod-product-compliance
Lightning Source LLC
LaVergne TN
LVHW012049070526
838201LV00082B/3875